D1518876

ANIMALS ON THE FARM

Goats

by Christina Leighton

BELLWETHER MEDIA • MINNEAPOLIS, MN

Note to Librarians, Teachers, and Parents:

Blastoff! Readers are carefully developed by literacy experts and combine standards-based content with developmentally appropriate text.

Level 1 provides the most support through repetition of high-frequency words, light text, predictable sentence patterns, and strong visual support.

Level 2 offers early readers a bit more challenge through varied simple sentences, increased text load, and less repetition of high-frequency words.

Level 3 advances early-fluent readers toward fluency through increased text and concept load, less reliance on visuals, longer sentences, and more literary language.

Level 4 builds reading stamina by providing more text per page, increased use of punctuation, greater variation in sentence patterns, and increasingly challenging vocabulary.

Level 5 encourages children to move from "learning to read" to "reading to learn" by providing even more text, varied writing styles, and less familiar topics.

Whichever book is right for your reader, Blastoff! Readers are the perfect books to build confidence and encourage a love of reading that will last a lifetime!

This edition first published in 2018 by Bellwether Media, Inc.

No part of this publication may be reproduced in whole or in part without written permission of the publisher. For information regarding permission, write to Bellwether Media, Inc., Attention: Permissions Department, 5357 Penn Avenue South, Minneapolis, MN 55419.

Library of Congress Cataloging-in-Publication Data

Names: Leighton, Christina.
Title: Goats / by Christina Leighton.
Description: Minneapolis, MN : Bellwether Media, Inc., 2018. | Series:
   Blastoff! Readers. Animals on the Farm | Includes bibliographical
   references and index. | Audience: Ages 5 to 8. | Audience: K to Grade 3.
Identifiers: LCCN 2017029510 | ISBN 9781626177239 (hardcover : alk. paper) | ISBN 9781681035031 (ebook)
Subjects: LCSH: Goats–Juvenile literature.
Classification: LCC SF383.35 .L45 2018 | DDC 636.3/9–dc23
LC record available at https://lccn.loc.gov/2017029510

Editor: Rebecca Sabelko   Designer: Lois Stanfield

Printed in the United States of America, North Mankato, MN.

Table of Contents

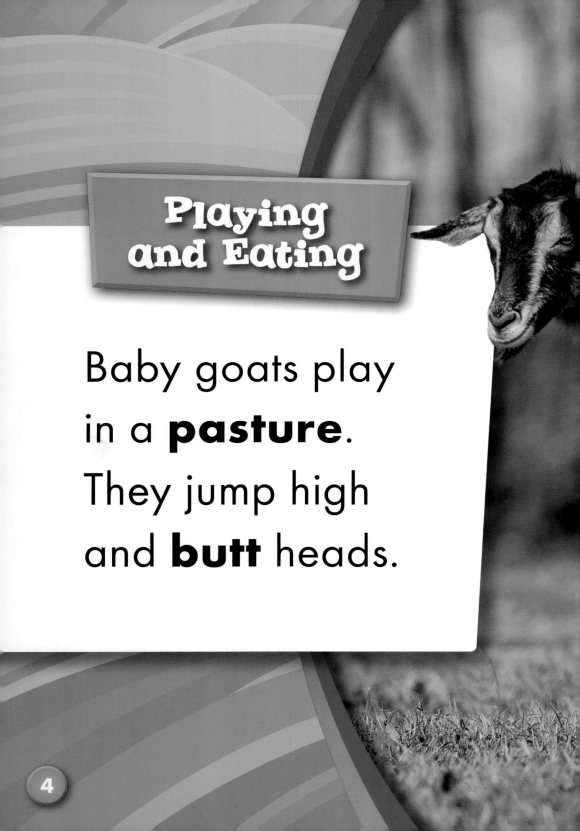

Playing and Eating

Baby goats play in a **pasture**. They jump high and **butt** heads.

Then they run to the barn. They **bleat** happily. The farmer left them hay!

What Are Goats?

Goats are friendly **mammals**. They come in many sizes and colors.

NAMES:

males: bucks
females: nannies
babies: kids

These animals have **split hooves**. They can easily move on different types of ground.

split
hooves

Goats may have straight or curved **horns**. Some have beards.

horns

beard

13

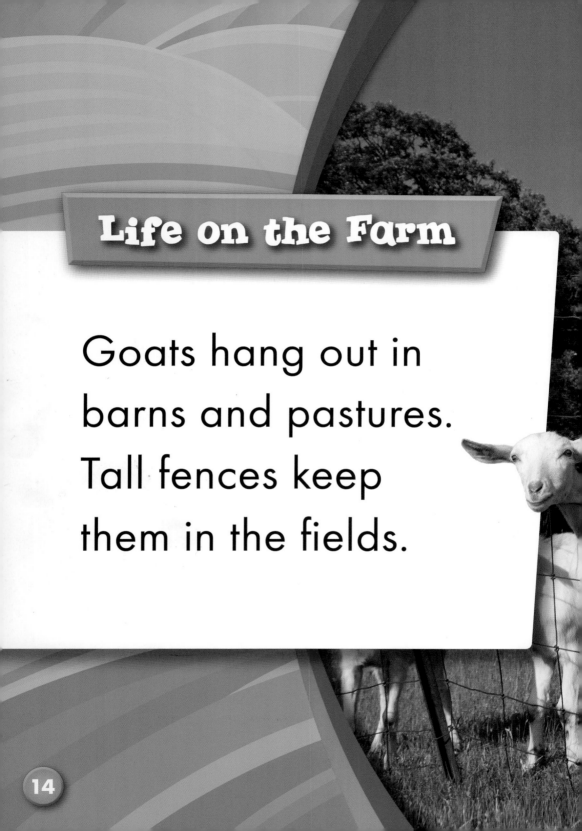

Life on the Farm

Goats hang out in barns and pastures. Tall fences keep them in the fields.

These mammals can eat almost anything! They may even eat hard twigs.

FAVORITE FOODS:

hay, twigs, weeds

17

Many goats
help farmers.
They eat weeds
and give milk.

farmer milking
a goat

19

These animals also get into trouble. Sometimes, goats open gates on their own!

Glossary

bleat

the sound a goat makes; a bleat sounds like a shaky cry.

mammals

warm-blooded animals that have hair and feed their young milk

butt

to hit with the top of the head

pasture

a large field where goats can feed on grasses and play

horns

hard, bony parts on the heads of some goats

split hooves

hard foot coverings that are divided into two parts

To Learn More

AT THE LIBRARY

Murray, Julie. *Goats*. Minneapolis, Minn.:
Abdo Kids, 2016.

Riggs, Kate. *Goats*. Mankato, Minn.: Creative
Education and Creative Paperbacks, 2017.

Schuetz, Kari. *Baby Goats*. Minneapolis,
Minn.: Bellwether Media, 2014.

ON THE WEB

Learning more about goats
is as easy as 1, 2, 3.

1. Go to www.factsurfer.com.

2. Enter "goats" into the search box.

3. Click the "Surf" button and you will see a
   list of related web sites.

With factsurfer.com, finding more information
is just a click away.

Index

DATE DUE

			PRINTED IN U.S.A.